# DEZIREE SAFARIS

*what is the difference between exploring and being lost?*

*" The Journey is the Destination..."*

*" free at last " Safari Company...*

TEAM DEZIREE
★ BOX 53441 ★
NAIROBI, KENYA.

New York London Nairobi Rome Yokohama Paris

# THE JOURNEY IS THE DESTINATION

**CHRONICLE BOOKS**
SAN FRANCISCO

# THE JOURNEY IS THE DESTINATION
## THE JOURNALS OF DAN ELDON

Edited by Kathy Eldon

THIS BOOK IS LOVINGLY DATED TO MY INSPIRATION,
AMY LOUISE ELDON

Library of Congress Cataloging-in-Publication Data available.
ISBN 0-8118-1586-2

Designed by Laura Lovett
Printed in Hong Kong

Distributed in Canada by
Raincoast Books
8680 Cambie Street
Vancouver, B.C. V6P 6M9

10 9 8 7 6 5 4 3

Chronicle Books
85 Second Street
San Francisco, CA  94105

www.chroniclebooks.com

My son, Dan Eidon, a Reuters photographer, was stoned to death in Somalia in July 1993 by a mob reacting to the United Nations bombing raid on the suspected headquarters of General Mohammed Farah Aidid. Only twenty-two when he died, Dan had already achieved prominence for his work as a war photographer. But his photographs told only half the story. The other half lay hidden away in seventeen black-bound journals filled with collages, writings, drawings, and photographs.

I was intensely proud of what I was allowed to see in the pages of Dan's journals, but I could never understand why he confined his artistic expression to the inside of books. Often I would ask him to produce works I could put on my walls. But Dan would always refuse, sometimes quite indignantly, and return to his black-bound journals, books he shared with only the closest of friends or family. By the time of his death, Dan had filled seventeen volumes, creating thousands of pages reflecting his own peculiar perspective on life. Layered like an archaeological dig, the pages are bizarre and colorful relics of a multifaceted civilization, intensely personal though inhabited by many different people.

# INTRODUCTION

Dan was born in England in 1970. (His father, Mike Eldon, is British. I am American.) From the very beginning of his life, his world was filled with color, pictures, and excitement: I dangled homemade mobiles above his cradle and surrounded him with an ever-changing display of greeting cards and drawings. Later, I stitched books and toys out of cloth and designed little puzzles, which Mike helped me cut out of wood for Dan and his little sister, Amy, born in 1974.

When our son was two and a half, we enrolled him at a Rudolph Steiner School, which emphasized the importance of music and art for young children. I remember one day standing at the door, rapt, as Dan and his tiny friends, engulfed in navy blue smocks, silently swirled watercolors on wet paper, swaying in time to classical music.

When Dan was seven, we moved from the orderly gray streets of suburban London to the chaos and riotous color of Nairobi. Under a spreading jacaranda tree in our garden, the children and I hammered together a playhouse out of a packing crate and painted dazzling flowers and animals on the sides. Our first houseguest helped draw a huge map of the world on Dan's bedroom wall, and Dan spent hours adding lions, elephants, and wildebeests onto the continent of Africa.

During our early days in Kenya, I led the children on magical safaris in the long grass of our garden, pointing out imaginary animals and people as we created whimsical stories which left us in fits of giggles.

Although oppressed by his British prep school, where errant boys were beaten with an old shoe, Dan was able to roam free with his friend, Lengai Croze, a white Kenyan who taught Dan to understand Africa. Lengai lived with his brother Anselm and sister Katrinika in a jumble of mud domes near the Nairobi Game Park. His mother, Nani, was a mural and stained glass designer with an incurable urge to decorate everything in sight. Even their minibus was covered with outrageous mythical creatures. An exotic menagerie, including geese and vultures, a colobus monkey, various iguanas, a herd of ostrich, and a pair of camels, lived in the Croze compound. Lengai and Dan loved exploring the bush around their *boma* like their heroes, Burton and Speke. The boys dangled from vines over the gorge that cut through the land and made friends with Masai children living nearby. On one of his walks, Dan encountered a buffalo. He escaped being gored by climbing a tree, but from that day on, a buffalo was his symbol of ultimate evil.

Meanwhile, Amy had found her own best friend, Lara Leakey, granddaughter of the great paleontologists Louis and Mary Leakey. Lara lived with her parents—and the threat of marauding lions—in a tiny mud house miles from the next neighbor. Marilyn Kelly, half-Kikuyu and half American, lived in town and went to ballet with Amy. The three little girls spent much of their time trying to trick Dan and Lengai into letting them climb into a massive treehouse we built in the backyard.

At the age of eleven, Dan refused to return to the English academy. We transferred him to the more informal International School of Kenya, set on a rambling campus high in the coffee fields outside Nairobi. With students from forty-six nations, it seemed that nearly every one of Dan's new friends was from a different country. Each child shared a new perspective of the world with his or her classmates, creating a dynamic atmosphere that encouraged curiosity and creativity.

When Dan was fourteen, his class went on an outing to the Loita Hills, home of the Loita clan of the Masai tribe of Kenya. Asked to produce a scrapbook of the adventure, he returned home with photographs and drawings of the Masai warriors and their wives and children. In addition, he had filled his pockets with shreds of feathers, ostrich shell fragments, old coins, beads, jewelry, leather thongs, and other treasures. Using everything he had collected, Dan produced a magical scrapbook in which each element found a place in an integrated whole. But nothing was as it had been. The photographs were cut into pieces, the drawings reassembled, feathers trimmed to fit the borders of the pages, and the beaded jewelry shaped to create whimsical frames for the images. Each page was overlaid with watercolors, markers, ink, even smudges of blood. The effect was dazzling. It was as though his spirit had been released in his art.

His next book was hardbound, retrieved from a heap of my old drawing books. The work in this book was bigger and far bolder. Dan experimented with every kind of material he could lay his hands on, working the pages over and over to achieve the effect he wanted, then starting over again on the next page with a completely new technique. The pages are luminous, filled with light and color, but using almost exclusively the African motifs he saw around him. Amy and Marilyn

made their first appearance in this book, and soon earned their status as Dan's favorite, and most compliant, models.

Dan made friends with a Masai family who lived twenty miles outside Nairobi on a barren, windy ridge nestled on the edge of the great Rift Valley. Kipenget, the mother of the family, struggled to feed her children by making beaded jewelry. Dan became her biggest buyer, hitching rides to visit her hut, always bearing gifts of sugar and tea. He wandered the hills with his young Masai "age-mates" before returning to town, arms filled with bags of jewelry. No one was safe for the next few weeks. Soon, every teacher and student at his school wore Kipenget's bracelets and necklaces, and I was pressed into service selling the jewelry to tourists and overseas visitors. Dan was always working to help other people, finding new and unusual ways to offer support. When Dan was fourteen, he learned that a young Kenyan child had a serious heart condition and required surgery. Immediately, he organized his friends to raise money, designing boxer shorts and tee shirts, and setting up bake sales and a series of wild dances in a hut in our back garden. The operation was successful, but the child, Atieno, died after contracting malaria in the local government hospital.

Throughout Dan's school years, I worked as a free-lance journalist for the *Nation,* the largest English language newspaper in Kenya. Dan often accompanied me on my interviews, and received the first of many photo credits in the paper at the age of fourteen. I encouraged him to find his own important stories to tell, both in words and pictures. Eventually, Dan's drawings and photographs threatened to overtake nearly everything in our house: the walls of his room, the margins of his homework, shirts, hats, cupboards, even a refrigerator door. As a senior in high school, he became the art director for the stodgy school newspaper, transforming it into a witty, avant-garde publication which narrowly missed being shut down by the school administration.

When Dan was seventeen, I left home and moved to London. Dan also left Africa to work as a design intern at *Mademoiselle* magazine in New York. His journal reflects his confusion at our family's dissolution, his resulting distrust of women, and the extreme sense of alienation he felt in the city. His images are hard-edged, cold and industrial, bustling and cynical, though sometimes nostalgically overlaid with lyrical silhouettes of dancing figures, buffaloes, and wildebeest. In New York his  darker side emerged, and he often flirted with danger in the rougher parts of town, where he liked to photograph homeless kids, street people, and gang members, with whom he had an immediate rapport. Our relationship was difficult. He worried about me, but always told me he was proud that I had been brave and did what I knew I had to do.

Three months later, Dan fled back to Nairobi, where he bought a seventeen-year-old Land Rover from an Australian traveler. He named the rusting hulk Deziree, paying tribute to the memory of a wild Italian girlfriend, and together with his friends Lengai and Patrick Falconer, set off on a great safari through Kenya, Tanzania, Malawi, Mozambique, and Zimbabwe. The intrepid explorers photographed themselves with Pygmies, battled impossible roads, sampled dried rats, bribed hostile border guards, and endured the threats of guerrillas. Their journey was a rollicking adventure—until they chanced upon a vast camp for displaced Mozambiquan refugees in Malawi. Stunned by the poverty and inspired by the irrepressible spirit of the people, who had virtually nothing, they vowed to return one day with tools for the refugees to help themselves.

Patrick and Lengai abandoned the safari at Victoria Falls to return to their universities, while Dan traveled alone from Malawi to Cape Town, taking advantage, as he wrote in his journal, of the "hospitality of South African jails" for accommodation. His journey is recorded in what has come to be called "Book Eight," a fat, mysterious volume of many layers, which begins with his analysis of the external world around him, and moves inexorably to an internal evaluation of his role as both observer and creator. This journal, above all others, is a private book. To make it difficult to read his words, he sometimes wrote in black ink on black paper, or red ink on a red background. He glued sheets of paper over great chunks of writing, leaving future readers only a few clues as to what he was thinking.

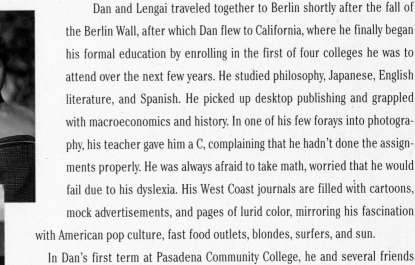

Dan and Lengai traveled together to Berlin shortly after the fall of the Berlin Wall, after which Dan flew to California, where he finally began his formal education by enrolling in the first of four colleges he was to attend over the next few years. He studied philosophy, Japanese, English literature, and Spanish. He picked up desktop publishing and grappled with macroeconomics and history. In one of his few forays into photography, his teacher gave him a C, complaining that he hadn't done the assignments properly. He was always afraid to take math, worried that he would fail due to his dyslexia. His West Coast journals are filled with cartoons, mock advertisements, and pages of lurid color, mirroring his fascination with American pop culture, fast food outlets, blondes, surfers, and sun.

In Dan's first term at Pasadena Community College, he and several friends founded a charity, Student Transport Aid, dedicated to helping the refugees fleeing Mozambique. Through a variety of ingenious (mostly legal) means, the group managed to raise $17,000. The following summer, together with thirteen young people, aged fifteen to twenty-two, he headed back to Africa. There, the group, representing seven different nationalities, purchased a Land Cruiser (named Arabella) to supplement Deziree on their safari. Their objective: the refugee camp in Malawi. Traveling south in Deziree and Arabella, the students encountered more challenges than rough roads, mercenaries, and bad maps. They had to learn how to get along together. Dan and Lengai fell in love with the same girl, beautiful Marte from Sweden, a devastating affair that he recorded with his usual ironic wit in a series of pages exploring "Agony and Remedy." Dan outlined his objectives—high and low—for the trip:

*Team Deziree: Free at Last Voyages, the Search for Clean Water in a Swamp: Mission Statement for Safari as a Way of Life*

*To explore the unknown and the familiar, distant and near, and to record, in detail with the eyes of a child, any beauty of the flesh or otherwise, horror, irony, traces of utopia or Hell.*

*Select your team with care, but when in doubt, take on new crew and give them a chance.*

*But avoid at all costs fluctuations of sincerity with your best people.*

In the margins he penciled a few more thoughts:

*Look for solutions, not problems.*

*It is therapeutic to apply a well toned naked body to one's flesh at least once a day in tropical and non-tropical climes.*

*The most important part of vehicle maintenance is clean windows, so if you are broken down you will enjoy the beauty of the view.*

The group arrived intact at the refugee camp. The students donated Arabella to the Save The Children Fund, gave money for two wells, and bought tools and blankets for the refugees. Each person was transformed by the safari, but no one was affected more than Dan, then aged nineteen.

Always restless, he plotted more safaris, and with each trip developed a greater proficiency in manipulating and distorting their record in his journal. He worked with glue, ink, photocopied images, and anything he could pick up along the way. Even without the benefit of computer tech-

nology, his images are startlingly multi-layered. In Japan he explored eroticism in ways he had never attempted before. His Moscow pages are hard and angry. In Marrakesh, he went slightly mad while waiting weeks for spare Land Rover parts, a state of mind reflected in the murky gray depths of his pages and the strange characters he photographed in the back streets, where few tourists ven-

tured. Constantly his pages asked and answered questions; the power of good versus evil, the role of violence in society, and the effect of war on humanity were recurring themes for him.

In April of 1992, Dan joined me to work as a third assistant director on a film set in Kenya, eagerly soaking up information from the Hollywood crew. He shot his own stills, among them surreal images of an achingly beautiful ash-daubed young Somali woman set against a stark background of black volcanic lava. The camera crew urged him to enroll in film school, recognizing in his photographs a potential director. I encouraged him to return to UCLA in the autumn and get a degree. Instead, he started a photography business in Nairobi, shooting ads for local newspapers and magazines. In his spare time he made a film, and always, he explored the world around him, hurriedly documenting everything he experienced. One girlfriend complained that he spent more time recording their relationship than actually enjoying it. He packed his hours with life, seemingly afraid to miss even a moment. Many people wondered then why he was always in such a hurry.

It was during that summer that Dan heard rumors of a famine in the Somali town of Baidoa. Together with a friend from the *Philadelphia Inquirer,* he drove north to see if there was any truth to the stories, discovering on their arrival that the famine was far worse than anyone had realized. Horrified, the pair photographed scores of dead babies, skeletal children, and hundreds of starving men and women. No longer speculating on the nature of man from a safe distance, Dan had to confront reality firsthand. His pictures were featured on the front pages of newspapers and magazines in many places, and were among the first to trigger the conscience of the world.

Something happened during that journey to irrevocably change Dan. He returned again and again to Somalia, inexorably drawn to the unfolding human drama he felt compelled to document. In a book about his experiences that he later self-published:

"After my first trip to Somalia, the terror of being surrounded by violence and the horrors of the famine threw me into a dark depression. Even journalists who had covered many conflicts were moved to tears. But for me, this was my first experience with war. Before Somalia, I had only seen two dead bodies in my life. I have now seen hundreds, tossed into ditches like sacks. The worst things I could not photograph.

"One Sunday morning, they brought in a pretty girl, wrapped in a colorful cloth. I saw that both her hands and feet had been severed by shrapnel. Someone had tossed a grenade in the market. She looked serene, like she was dead . . . but the nurse said she would survive. It made me think of the whole country. Somalia will survive, but what kind of life is it for a people that have been so wounded. I don't know how these experiences have changed me, but I feel different."

As the conflict intensified, Dan found himself in increasingly dangerous situations, but, having grown up in Kenya, he was aware of the risks, knew how to maneuver, and took great care, both for himself and others. In November of 1992, in an article entitled "Photography in Danger Zones" published in *Executive* magazine in Kenya, he wrote:

"The hardest situation to deal with is a frenzied mob, because they cannot be reasoned with. I try to appeal to one or two of the most sympathetic and restrained looking people with the most effective looking assault rifles, but I have realized that no photograph is worth my life."

With each trip back to Somalia, Dan grew closer to the people. Mischievous, cheerful, and very good at his job, he seemed to know everyone—aid workers, Marines, diplomats, and thieves. The locals dubbed him "the Mayor of Mogadishu," and children followed him down the potholed streets like the Pied Piper.

But he was increasingly frustrated with the tragic events unfolding before him, and he confessed to his friends that he was weary of the violence and killing.

I spoke to Dan when he called on my birthday, June 26. He was in Nairobi for a brief rest before returning to Mogadishu, where eighteen Pakistani peacekeepers had recently been murdered. I tried not to sound too anxious, but of course I was worried about his safety. I asked him if it wasn't time to come home.

"Please don't ask me to leave," he said. "My job isn't done. I have to stay." I remembered how he had supported me when I made the difficult decision to leave my home in Africa.

"Okay," I said. "I'm proud of you. No matter what, you're leading the life of your choice and I'm proud of you." We hung up quickly. Two minutes later, the telephone rang again. "I love you, Mum," he said hoarsely. "It's been too long. We need to talk."

Seventeen days later, on July 12, 1993, Dan and three colleagues, Hansi Krauss of the Associated Press and Anthony Macharia and Hos Maina of Reuters, were called to the scene of a brutal bombing by United Nations forces of a house believed to be the headquarters of General Aidid. When the photographers arrived at the compound and began shooting the bloody carnage, the crowd, enraged at the death or mutilation of over a hundred people, including religious leaders and respected elders of the community, turned on the journalists, stoning and beating them to death. In a moment of horrific irony, Dan and his friends were murdered by the very people they were trying to help.

One week later, we gathered together on Kipenget's land to celebrate Dan's life. Billowy clouds hung in a perfect sky as a crowd of many hundreds found places on the grass before a makeshift altar decorated with flowers, African cloth, and one of Dan's collection of funny hats. Dan's friends of every shade and color, religion and creed, joined together in a ceremony of peace in a place more beautiful than any cathedral on earth.

There were many tears that day when Dan's journalist colleagues struggled to find words for their horror. As people talked, we could hear the sound of cattle and goats being herded back to their homes by young Masai children and watched the occasional Land Rover hug the narrow road along the edge of the Ngong Hills.

The sun was setting when Amy stood to read a letter from Lengai. Amy was determined to get through the letter, though she said later that she felt as though the light of her life had gone out.

After Amy read Lengai's words, we then lit ten torches to set alight a fire to commemorate the sparks Dan lit in others, as an African choir sang, "Let there be peace on earth . . . the peace that was meant to be." People cried again, not just for Dan, but for a world gone wrong.

Not long afterwards someone brought us a rucksack of Dan's belongings, retrieved from his hotel room in Mogadishu. In it we found Dan's last journal. Whereas all the books he had kept before included collages, whimsical drawings, and fanciful images, the Somali journal is stark and simple, nothing but photographs stuck on pages. Like his life, it is unfinished, the photographs standing as mute but powerful reminders of a life that ended too soon.

KATHY ELDON
Los Angeles, 1997

Spent the night with my friend
Lengai who lives just outside of
the game park. I drove out there
after school with his mother. We
rode his new motor bike and looked
at his animals. He has a serval
cat, two vultures, a horse, lots
of dogs and cats and a crested
crane. Their generator was broken
so I had to do my homework
with a ~~candle~~. lantern.

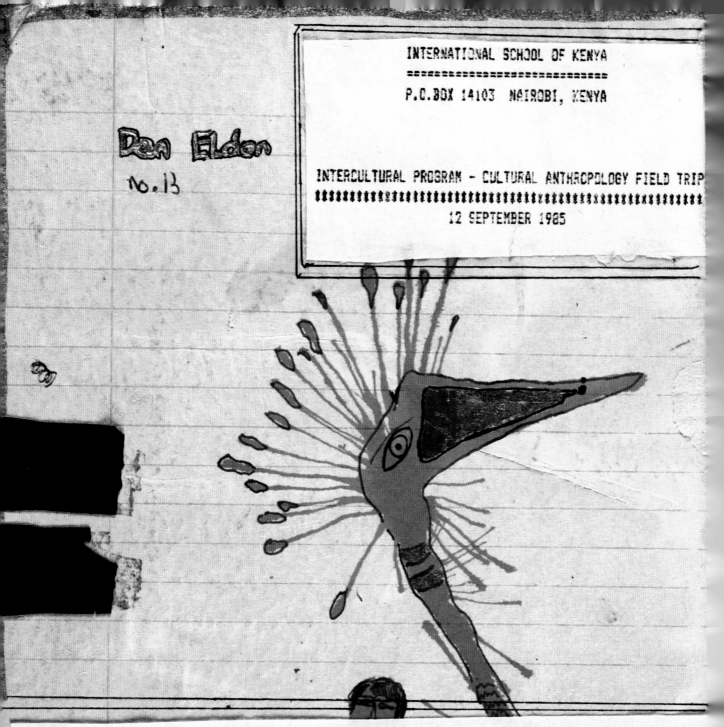

Dan Eldon
No. 13

INTERNATIONAL SCHOOL OF KENYA
P.O.BOX 14103  NAIROBI, KENYA

INTERCULTURAL PROGRAM - CULTURAL ANTHROPOLOGY FIELD TRIP
12 SEPTEMBER 1985

"WHENEVER POSSIBLE THE ETHNOLOGIST BECOMES ETHNOGRAPHER BY GOING OUT TO LIVE AMONG THE PEOPLE UNDER STUDY.  BY EATING THEIR FOOD, SPEAKING THEIR LANGUAGE, AND PERSONALLY OBSERVING THEIR HABITS AND CUSTOMS, THE ETHNOGRAPHER IS ABLE TO UNDERSTAND A SOCIETY'S WAY OF LIFE TO A FAR GREATER EXTENT THAN ANY "ARMCHAIR ANTHROPOLOGIST" EVER COULD; ONE LEARNS A CULTURE BEST BY LEARNING HOW TO BEHAVE ACCEPTABLY ONESELF IN THE SOCIETY IN WHICH ONE IS DOING FIELDWORK.  THE ETHNOGRAPHER TRIES TO BECOME A PARTICIPANT-OBSERVER IN THE CULTURE UNDER STUDY.  [THIS DOES NOT MEAN THAT MILK MIXED WITH BLOOD HAS TO BE DRUNK IN ORDER TO STUDY THE MAASAI.  BUT BY LIVING AMONG MAASAI, THE ETHNOGRAPHER SHOULD BE ABLE TO UNDERSTAND THE ROLE OF THE BLOOD/MILK MIXTURE IN THE OVERALL CULTURAL SCHEME.]  HE OR SHE MUST BE A METICULOUS OBSERVER IN ORDER TO BE ABLE TO GET A BROAD OVERVIEW WITHOUT PLACING UNDUE STRESS ON ANY OF ITS COMPONENT PARTS.  ONLY BY DISCOVERING HOW ALL SOCIAL INSTITUTIONS - POLITICAL, ECONOMIC, RELIGIOUS - FIT TOGETHER CAN THE ETHNOGRAPHER BEGIN TO UNDERSTAND THE CULTURAL SYSTEM."

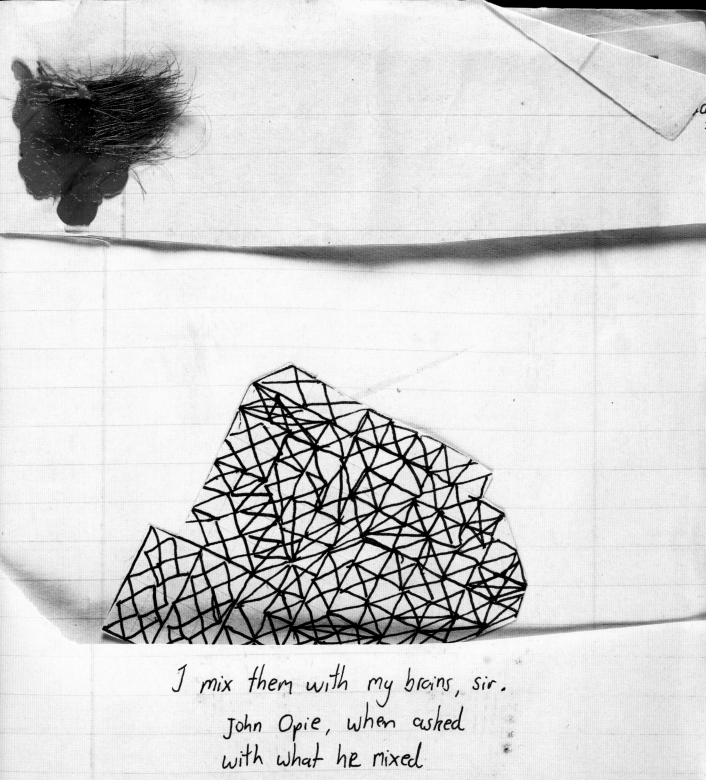

I mix them with my brains, sir.
John Opie, when asked
with what he mixed
his colours.

love
+kisses
Angela

Love

ANGELA FISHER
TRADITIONAL JEWELRY LTD

6 Caledonia Place
Weighbridge
St Helier
Jersey
Channel Islands
Phone 0534 20266

42 Belsize Avenue
London NW3
England
Phone 01 435-1919

MORE VOLUME ON THAT SPEAKER, MIKE! IT GONNA NEED IT!!!

TOWN
HURLINGHAM
NDEMI CLOSE
SECOND GATE ON RIGHT, OFF NDEMI CLOSE
NDEMI RD.
ELDON
ADAMS ARCADE
ROAD
Kingara St. Askaris?

MIKE AND JOHNS MKEBE MIX

BIG AUDIO VISUAL DYNAMITI!!

aMORPhoUS !¡D
ANARCHY iN tHE MKEBE
(With cLAuDiUS GEtLOoR F) i ?%$

EXPERIENCE!!

FROM EIGHTISH TO ONEISH FOOD: ONE MKEBE HAPPY MEAL FREE

50/-

MARCH 17

# THANKYOU!LE

THANK YOU FOR BUYING AN INVITATION TO THE MKEBE. THE MONEY THAT WE RAISE, WILL BE USED TO PAY HOSPITAL BILLS FOR ATIENO GABRIEL, A 17 YEAR OLD GIRL, WHO URGENTLY NEEDS SURGERY ON HER HEART. YOUR DONATION WILL BE OF GREAT IMPORTANCE DURING THE TIME THAT SHE STAYS IN NAIROBI HOSPITAL AFTER THE OPERATION, AND WHILE SHE REGIANS HER STRENGTH AND STAMMINA.

MKEBE

IN THE RAIN

THE MKEBE

# MAGENDO

# BROTHERS

SAMBURU

И ВСЕХ СТРАН, СОЕДИНЯЙТЕСЬ! ПРОЛЕТАРІ ВСІХ КРАЇН, ЄДНАЙТЕСЯ! ПРАЛЕТАРЫ ЎСІХ КРАЁН, ЯДНАЙЦЕСЯ! БУТУН ДУНЁ...

АДЕРДІН ПРОЛЕТАРЛАРЫ, БІРІГІҢДЕР! ᲞᲠᲝᲚᲔᲢᲐᲠᲔᲑᲘ ᲧᲕᲔᲚᲐ ᲥᲕᲔᲧᲜᲘᲡᲐ, ᲨᲔᲔᲠᲗᲓᲘᲗ! БУТУН ӨЛКӘЛӘРИН ПРОЛ...

...ДИН ТОАТЕ ЦЭРИЛЕ, УНИЦИ-ВЭ! VISU ZEMJU PROLETĀRIEŠI, SAVIENOJIETIES! БАРДЫК Е...

...НАМЛАКАТХО, ЯК ШАВЕД! ᲤᲠᲝᲚᲔᲑᲐᲠᲘᲐᲚᲐᲠ ᲠᲐᲒᲐᲠ ᲮᲠᲐᲮᲮᲘᲠᲐ, ᲘᲠᲐᲕᲡᲘ* ӘХЛИ ЮРТЛАРЫҢ ПРОЛЕТАРЫ...

## ИЗ...
### СОВЕТОВ Н...

Газета выходит с марта 1917 года

(21918) ◆     Вторник, 21 апреля 1987     Цена

— Интервью с героем снимка —

# ...ТЬ НА ПЕРЕДНЕМ
# ...БЕЖЕ ПЕРЕСТРОЙКИ

## ФАКТОР
## ДОВЕРИЯ

...ии Новго-
...о Совета
...немало
...сказано о
...е Проши-
... впервые
...городского
...завода де-
...о райсове-
...е выборы

...ял общую
...ошёл в го-
... — они жи-
...улице По-
...хсот пяти-
...аждой зна-
...приема, а
...рь: «Здрав-
...брали, что

...к непри-
...! В ручке
...лась, а ли-
...сли запи-
...записывал
...ии, советы,
...ще, дол-
...жен сказать, что, может быть,
...именно такие встречи и дают

друг другу, а доверие в моей
работе — очень важный фак-
тор.

жителей дома или домов за-
слушиваем отчеты должност-
ных лиц жилищно-эксплуата-

собственно, никто и
теперь «отписывать-
дами образовался

...ым молодым за всю
...комсомольских съез-
...сле делегатов — спе-

ного переустройства.
Прочно опираясь на лучшие
традиции, демократический

Susheela Roach

Dana Schmidt

...ontan

Rajnesh Shah     Neha Shahar

Katherine Sindling    Alan Stevenson

## Junior Class Officers

Left to right : Chris Cram, Robin Canon, Johnathon Bernard, Brad Coleman.

Mattia Takahashi    Eric Taylor    Julian Van den Rike    Elsa Walker

Rena Alberto    Lisa Atkins    Lisa Beckloff    Zebb Bekere

A thousand colour TVs, mor...
than 700 radio receivers and tap...
recorders, 2,600 amateur fil...
and photo cameras, more tha...
2,500 vacuum cleaners, abou...
12,000 watches and many oth...
household appliances come o...
the conveyer daily
at Leningrad
enterprises.

SEPT 1987

extract from the Koran. page 73 -the bit about topless sun- bathing.

Last photograph of Baron Von Grangers daughters before their execution. Frauline Darla (left) comforts her sister Dawn (right) moments before she is taken to be beheaded. October 3rd 1914. 5 p.m. - My film was removed after I took this picture and was only returned after I gave the sentry my pocket watch.

Frauline Dawn Von Granger is prepared for the execution by a palace slave. I was unable to aid her as she was under constant supervision from palace guards at all times.

Dawn lies fallen but head still intact. It took 17 blows to dislodge her head from the neck.

Daughter of the sheikh and slave October, 1914

Photographs taken in Royal tent before the camel races and sheep eye feast.

Note short curved dagger - rhino horn handle

Coins presented to me by the sheikh himself before cutting my hand off. Note rare Islamic markings on outer ridge of coin. These coins were minted by Sheikh Abu Kamu in 1512 to commemorate his twenty fifth wife.

Before anyone could fire a shot, the men decided to

continued →

chamber MAID
Ethiopia

## Опасные предметы и вещества

В целях обеспечения безопасности пассажирам запрещается перевозить как при себе, так и в багаже нижеперечисленные опасные предметы и вещества:

**Сжатые газы** – горючие, негорючие или ядовитые: бытовой газ, бутан, кислород, пропан, заряженные баллоны аквалангистов;

Цилиндры со сжатым газом

Заряженные баллоны аквалангистов

**Едкие вещества** – кислоты, щелочи, аккумуляторные батареи, ртуть и аппараты, содержащие ртуть;

Аккумуляторные батареи

**Взрывчатые вещ**
снаряжение, пироте
сигнальные ракеты

Револьверы

Боеприпасы
пустые пат

Пистолетные
пистоны

**Легковоспламен**
**и твердые веще**
зажигалок и нагрева
ковозгораемые вещ

Разовые
зажигалки

Спички пассажиры могут иметь при себе

**Радиоактивные**

Портфели и атта

бы сделали хороший выбо
эрофлот предлагает пре
словия для деловых и ту
утешествий, гарантирует
остеприимство.
лагодарим за полет!

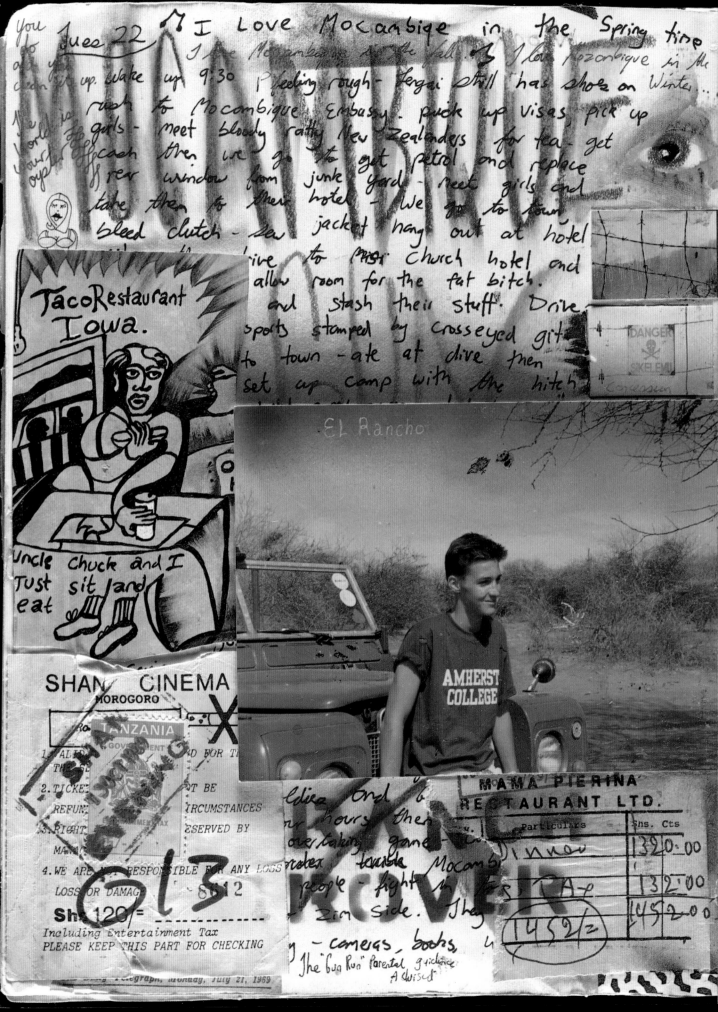

You ... Tues 22 ♪ I Love Moçambique in the Spring time ... I love Mozambique in the fall ... ♪ I love Mozambique in the clean it up. Wake up 9:30 feeling rough - Sergei still has shits on winter... rush to Moçambique Embassy - pick up visas, pick up girls - meet bloody ratty New Zealanders for tea - get cash then we go to get petrol and replace rear window from junk yard - meet girls and take them to their hotel - We go to town bleed clutch - sew jacket hang out at hotel ... drive to church hotel and allow room for the fat bitch. and stash their stuff. Drive sports stamped by crosseyed git to town - ate at dive then set up camp with the hitch ...

TacoRestaurant Iowa.

Uncle Chuck and I Just sit and eat

EL Rancho

AMHERST COLLEGE

SHAN CINEMA
MOROGORO

TANZANIA
GOVERNMENT

1. ALL ... THE SE ... D FOR TH
2. TICKE ... T BE
REFUN ... IRCUMSTANCES
... ESERVED BY
3. RIGHT ...
MA ...
4. WE ARE ... RESPONSIBLE FOR ANY LOSS
LOSS OR DAMAGE ... 8512
Shs. 120/= ----------
Including Entertainment Tax
PLEASE KEEP THIS PART FOR CHECKING

... Telegraph, Monday, July 21, 1989

MAMA PIERINA
RESTAURANT LTD.

| Particulars | Shs. | Cts |
|---|---|---|
| Dinner | 1320 | 00 |
| ... | 132 | 00 |
| | 1452 | 00 |

idea and ... hours then overtaking game... rolex terrible Moçambi... people - fight in Zim side. They ... cameras, books, 4 ...
The "Bua Run" Parental Guidance Advised

LAND ROVER
G13

**Men travel miles to glimpse the notorious golden nude.**

The work of a photographer often requires him to manipulate young girls into different poses. But I must

remind critics that at no time do we think of any thing else but the Job on hand

Please don't look at this photo and want to slowly remove the cloth.

# MEET NANCY'S "FAMILY"

2nd Sept 1989

Wash and drink at Holiday Inn. Drive to Avondale, Italian bakery - eat pizza, go outside, find Italian guys on motorbikes there - they help try to fix starter - then "Innocen" and his gang of thieves come, they clean my points - still no start - drive back to town, pick up hitch hiker.

Find road to Nancy's place by Airport - meet her Mum and Dad, have some beer and talk for a few hours. Nancy and I are sent to get more beer from shop. Jane, Sinclair with us. Watch wrestling on T.V. - have wine and dinner good spicy stew. Other brother come, we go for a ride to buy bottles again with Mush. return and watch Kaak Kid video, see family albums, have hot bath, set up bed. - Wash clothes in car, leaky washing machine, push car against wall so there's no red lights - clean car out completely, fix back window

## X.T.C.!

Dress for church in tight trousers + Debbie with us to go not. - Drive to church, arrive late - bird trapped in church, have communion, I have no money for collection, Sinclair runs around causing trouble, sermon about sister is a lion waiting for christian impulse. Sermon about The adulteress who they were going to stone to death and Jesus said "let he who has committed no sin throw the first stone." everyone teased cruised and left Jesus and the woman alone and he said "no one else condemns you so neither do I, get out of here and start your life with out sin, go on, scram!" Meet people outside, they think Nancy's friend Tony return have meal and then drive to concession stop along the way at a Hotel - see old photos

Telegrams: "PROVINCER", Nairobi
Inquiries and all other offices—
Telephone: Nairobi 333551
When replying please quote

Ref. No. ............... CER 2/28 VOL II
        and date

PROVINCIAL COMMISSIONER
NAIROBI AREA
P.O. Box 30124
NAIROBI

............24th MAY..., 19...89

A.D'Cunha,
P.O. BOX 53441,
NAIROBI.

RE: STAFF DINNER PARTY

Permission is hereby granted to you to hold the above mentioned party
on 26th May,1989  at ~~the~~ residence, Maikipia road, Kileleshwa  /your
starting from 6.00 P.M. to midnight.

Ensure law and order is maintained.

703 73 16 1-13

F. T. KIMEMIA
FOR: PROVINCIAL COMMISSIONER
NAIROBI AREA

cc.

The District Officer
Parklands Division
NAIROBI.

The O.C.S,
Kilimani police station
NAIROBI.

"Hey, G.I., you WANT JAPANESE
Girl Frein'?"

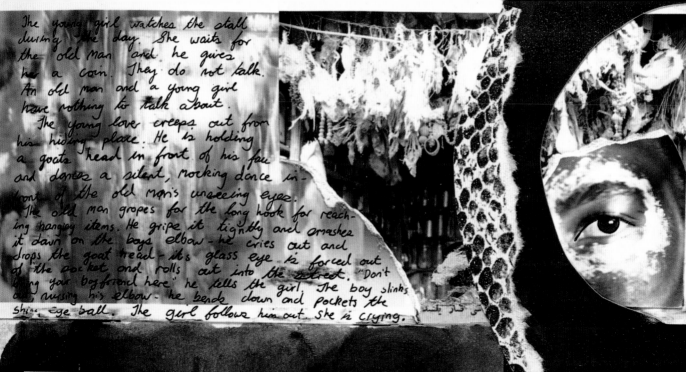

The young girl watches the stall during the day. She waits for the old man and he gives her a coin. They do not talk. An old man and a young girl have nothing to talk about.

The young love creeps out from his hiding place. He is holding a goats head in front of his face and dances a silent, mocking dance in front of the old man's unseeing eyes.

The old man gropes for the long hook for reaching hanging items. He grips it tightly and smashes it down on the boys elbow - he cries out and drops the goat head - its glass eye is forced out of the pocket and rolls out into the street. "Don't bring your boyfriend here" he tells the girl. The boy slinks out, nursing his elbow - he bends down and pockets the shiny eye ball. The girl follows him out. She is crying.

The Baby Owl is the blind man's only friend. He puts his hand on the cage and whispers "you have eyes enough for both of us my friend. The baby Owl has been in the shop since the old man first put him there - over twelve years - when customers ask "How can a bird be a chick for twelve whole years, the wise, old man always replies "all is not as it "how can a man be ___ for Looks" his whole life"?

He old is kept in cage with Carmen The baby bend a to end bird to easily.

Deziree.

I had been following the blind man since he left the Mosque. I have a obsession with the blind because my world is 100 percent visual. I always follow a blind person if I have time. I enter his shop...

# UNITED NATIONS ENVIRONMENT PROGRAMME

# GEMS

### THE GLOBAL ENVIRONMENT MONITORING SYSTEM
### PROGRAMME ACTIVITY CENTRE

Your Reference:

Our Reference:

8 August 1989

To Whom It May Concern

EMBASSY OF THE
UNITED STATES OF AMERICA

P
Lil

To Whom It May Concern:

Mr. Daniel Robert Eldon,
holder of regular passp
American Embassy in Lilo
to Kenya via Tanzania.
border post in Mbeya and

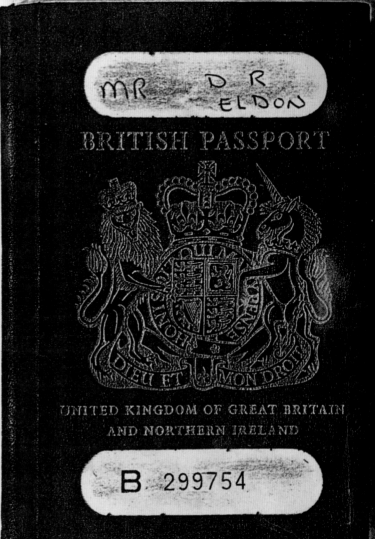

I approached Dr. Croze in London and suggested that we meet in the city to discuss what I called a "matter of some interest" Dr. Croze was free from academic responsibility because the silly bastard had just been booted out of school for climbing on the roof.

We agreed to meet at Pizza Hut and it was there that I proposed the idea of an expidition penetrating deep into the African bush. Dr. Croze was immediately receptive to the idea of another Pizza Americano but was hesitant to respond to my proposition. "Good Lord, Eldon, do you know what you're suggesting? Are you serious." he queried.

"My dear boy" I responded, "I have never been more serious In my entire life." Croze sensed the urgency in my tone of voice... the time was right. I withdrew the Map of Africa from my tunic and clapped it down on the pizza in front of Dr. Croze. He slowly inserted the monicle into his eye and unfolded the enormous map onto the table and onto the table of the six skin-headed gentlemen adjacent to ourselves. "Oi, watch yourself bogey face" they quipped as they stabbed a fork into the head of Dr. Croze. Dr. Croze, being a serious academic and a man of the church, was unused to such strong language and after smashing up the young hooligans we sat back down. Crozes face grew pink with glee as his pale, watery, onion coloured eyes traced the route that my long, elegant, aristocratic fingers pointed to. In fact it was after looking at the waitress that we got back to the map.

The plan was to drive my recently purchased Land Rover from Nairobi to as far south as humanly possible in a clapped out old Land Rover that was, in fact the same Land Rover that Napoleon used in the Battle of Midway Island in 1066.

We shook hands and Croze earnestly pledged that no matter what happened, I would pick up the bill for the pizzas.

We then proceeded to the bank where Dr. Croze grappled with the automatic cash machine. You must understand that Dr. Croze is very much an old world gentleman and unused to such modern affairs.

All we had to do now was to convince Lengai's dad to shell out the cash that would make the epic voya. possible

# Mandelo Ya Magi
## The gearbox removal

*Aieeeee! I've pulled it off!*

# "Soak it in Diesel"
# MOROGORO

*when in doubt...*

The Dutch Mechanic is reluctant to take us in but agrees and we (Lengai) get down to work, taking out seats, gear boxes. PX

**GEAR BOX**

Lengai becomes very quiet and works flat out alongside the mechanics he starts soaking everything in diesel, everything. The problem is located and fixed. It is only a roller bearing. We are lucky. That night we celebrate with Vodka and coke and Kebabs in down town Morogoro.

*I'd hate to think what that noise was.*

WAnkel Rotary engine

VODKA

Here, Dr. A.L. Croze shares a joke with Klaus Von Mercedes at their workshop in Munich. The Croze-Mercedez team would go on to invent the first internal combustion engine.

Munich 1902

Baron Klaus Von Mercedez.

Baron Von Mercedes never lived to see his invention. He was mysteriously "soaked in diesel"

The founding father of the Modern Automobile, Dr. A.L. Croze. O.B.E.

Repair outside tail/fact/carp.

| date | labor hours | in | out | total | Description of job: |
|---|---|---|---|---|---|

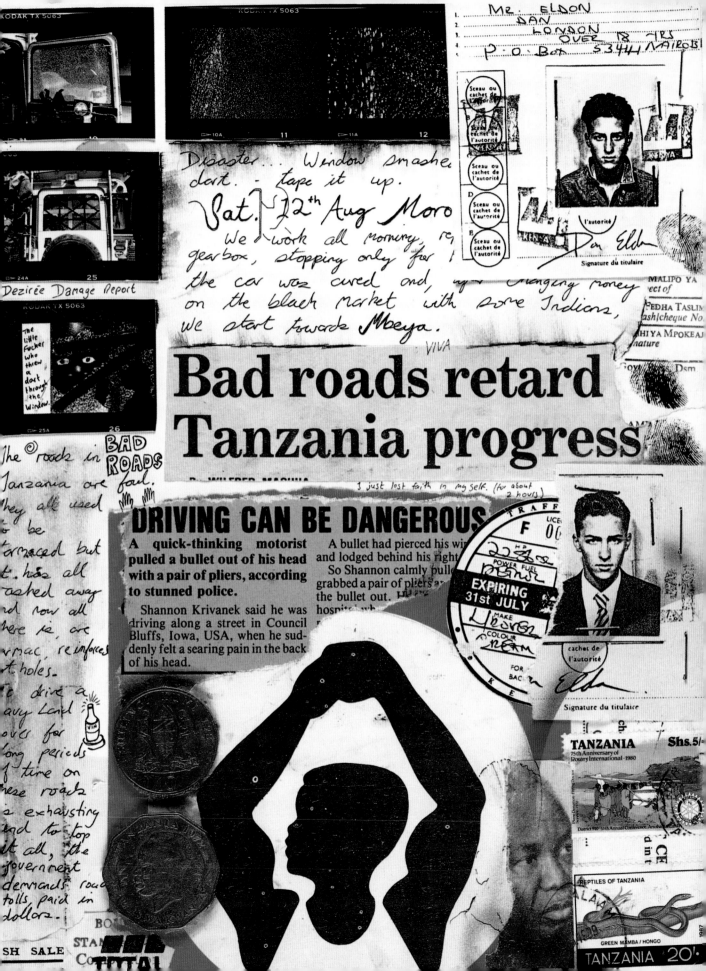

Disaster... Window smashed dark. - tape it up.

Sat. 12th Aug Moro

We work all morning, re gearbox, stopping only for the car was cured and, changing money on the black market with some Indians, we start towards Mbeya.

VIVA

Dezirèe Damage Report

The little Fucker who threw a dart through the window.

# Bad roads retard Tanzania progress
By WILFRED MASHULA

The roads in BAD ROADS Tanzania are foul. They all used to be tarmaced but it has all washed away and now all there is, are tarmac, reinforced pot holes. To drive a heavy Land over for long periods of time on these roads is exhausting and to top it all, the government demands road tolls, paid in dollars.

I just lost faith in my self. (for about 2 hours)

## DRIVING CAN BE DANGEROUS

A quick-thinking motorist pulled a bullet out of his head with a pair of pliers, according to stunned police.

Shannon Krivanek said he was driving along a street in Council Bluffs, Iowa, USA, when he suddenly felt a searing pain in the back of his head.

A bullet had pierced his win and lodged behind his right

So Shannon calmly pulle grabbed a pair of pliers a the bullet out. H hospital wh

EXPIRING 31st JULY

TANZANIA
75th Anniversary of Rotary International-1980

Shs.5/-

REPTILES OF TANZANIA

GREEN MAMBA / HONGO

TANZANIA 20/-

Under Article 29 a candidate shall be nominated for election as an Officer in the same manner as a Member of the Club is nominated for election to the Committee provided that any such candidate is, or shall have been, a serving member of the Committee or a former Officer.

immediately woke Dengai from his dreams of Angle tace and presented him
...th the snapped gear. He ...asked ... ... ... ... ... ...
...nce I was in no ...
...rdly stray from the...
...everal hours, so I...
...atrick and dove onto...

In the next few ...
...the cover of the gear...
...nto position with a...
...this and by the ...
...hite hot and indeed...
...moment for patrick ...
...and slept then at ...
...scalded fingers. It ...

## Sunday 13th Aug  Iringa, ...  NIGHT of the LIVING GEARBO...

After three hour sleep. Lengai decided that it was time to
wake up. We loaded Deziree into second gear. By this time
...re we had ...
...the engine a...
This involve...
or "some insi...
...in the engine...

We drove ...
some welders ...
gear. This ...
expect. It ...
the drivers ...
ventilation ...
glass window...
We drove...
marsh, untill...
series of va...

Deziree,
North Africa
1944, while on
use as Rommel's
staff car

Dr. Croze

Arusha - Mombo  The great Trek All Night

...We went off the road and bush-wacked down to the
edge of a cliff. The car was parked at a very
...akish angle. We proceeded to set up the most comprehensive
...ampsite. We set up our tables, chairs, tarp, lights, fire and patrick
... whipped up a rather tasty spagetti which we
ate in between many sips of rum and coke
which eventualy purged our camp of sobriety.
It was time to explore the cliffs and caverns
below.

...rade of pink, crumsly stone.

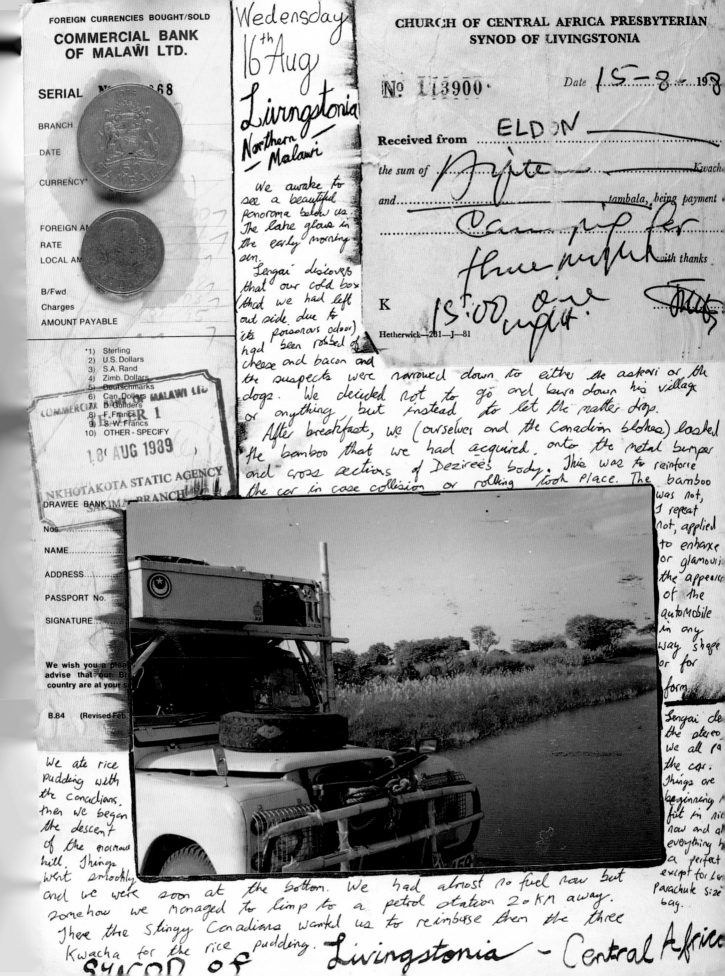

Wedensday
16th
Aug

Livingstonia
Northern
Malawi

We awoke to
see a beautiful
panorama below us.
The lake glows in
the early morning
air.
Lengai discovers
that our cold box
(that we had left
out side due to
its poisonous odour)
had been robbed of
cheese and bacon and
the suspects were narrowed down to either the askari or the
dogs. We decided not to go and burn down his village
or anything, but instead to let the matter drop.
After breakfast, we (ourselves and the Canadian blokes) lashed
the bamboo that we had acquired. onto the metal bumper
and cross sections of Deziree's body. This was to reinforce
the car in case collision or rolling took place. The bamboo
was not,
I repeat
not, applied
to enhance
or glamouri
the appearan
of the
automobile
in any
way shape
or for
form

Lengai de
the stereo
we all ra
the car
Things are
beginning
fit in ni
now and al
everything h
a perfect
except for Le
parachute size
bag.

We ate rice
pudding with
the canadians.
then we began
the descent
of the enormous
hill. Things
went smoothly
and we were soon at the bottom. We had almost no fuel now but
somehow we managed to limp to a petrol station 20 km away.
There the stingy Canadians wanted us to reimburse them the three
Kwacha for the rice pudding. Livingstonia — Central Africa

SYNOD OF

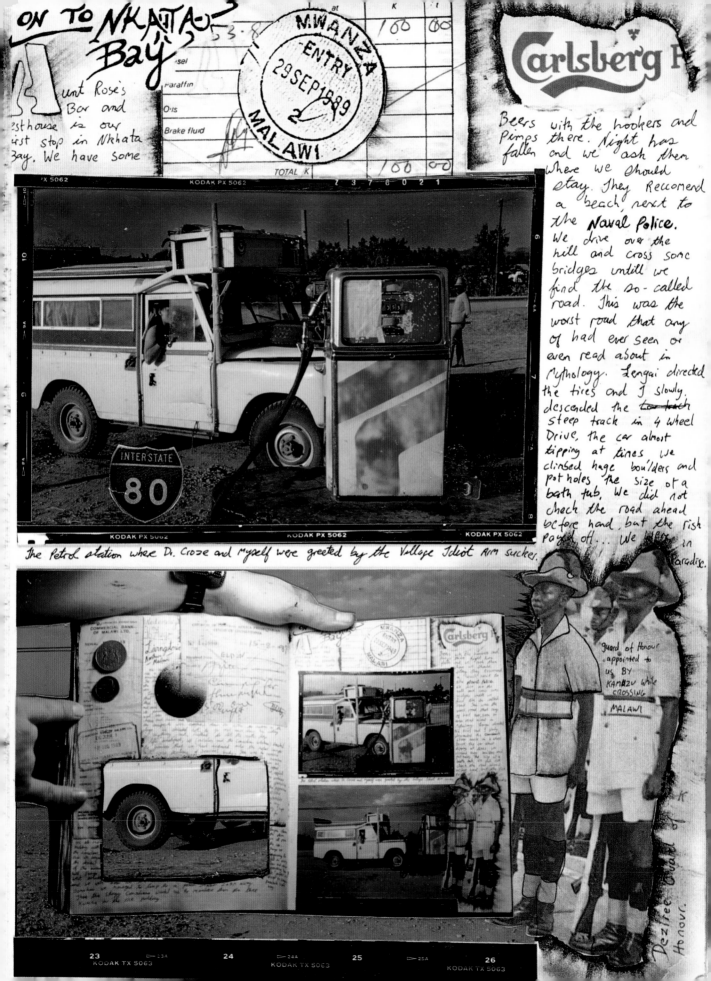

ON TO NKATA Bay

Aunt Rose's Bar and ...esthouse is our ...irst stop in Nkhata Bay. We have some

MWANZA ENTRY 29 SEP 1989 2 MALAWI

Carlsberg

Beers with the hookers and Pimps there. Night has fallen and we ask them where we should stay. They Recomend a beach, next to the Naval Police. We drive over the hill and cross some bridges untill we find the so-called road. This was the worst road that any of had ever seen or even read about in Mythology. Lengai directed the tires and I slowly descended the ~~too track~~ steep track in 4 wheel Drive, the car almost tipping at times we climbed huge boulders and potholes the size of a bath tub. We did not check the road ahead before hand, but the rish payed off... We ...... in Paradise.

INTERSTATE 80

The Petrol station where Dr. Croze and myself were greeted by the Village Idiot Arm sucker.

guard of Honour appointed to us BY KAMUZU while CROSSING MALAWI

← Read this and think about how weird some people are.

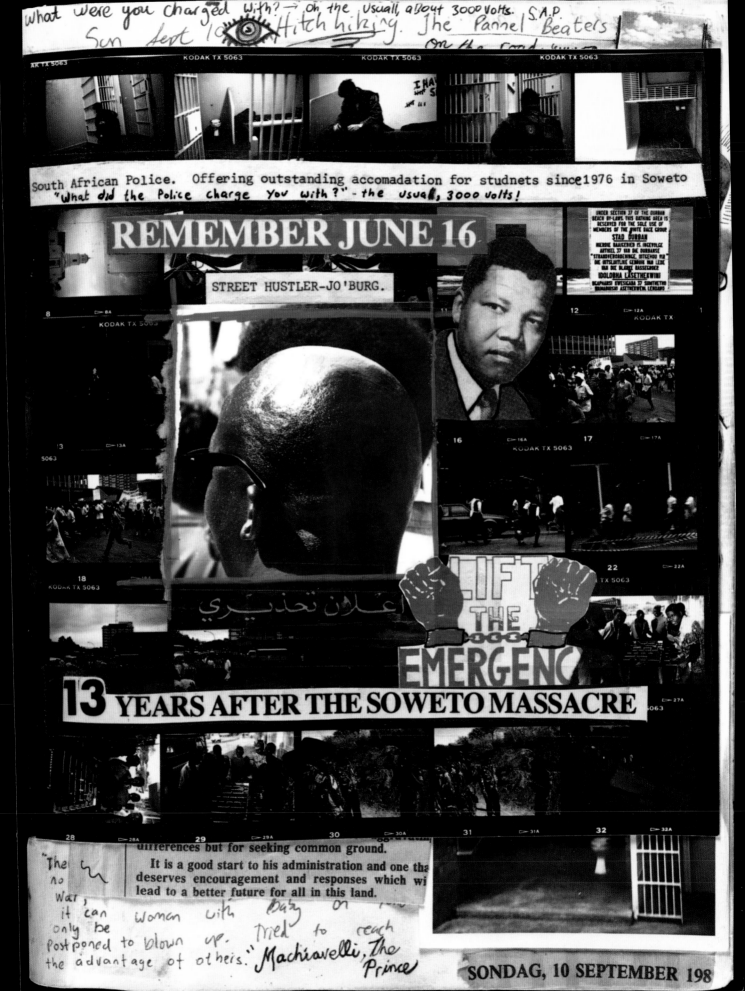

What were you charged with? – Oh the usuall, about 3000 volts. S.A.P.
Sun Sept 10. Hitchhiking. The Pannel Beaters on the road.

South African Police. Offering outstanding accomadation for studnets since 1976 in Soweto
"What did the Police charge you with?" – the usual, 3000 volts!

REMEMBER JUNE 16

STREET HUSTLER-JO'BURG.

اعلان تحذيري

LIFT THE EMERGENC

13 YEARS AFTER THE SOWETO MASSACRE

differences but for seeking common ground.

It is a good start to his administration and one tha deserves encouragement and responses which wi lead to a better future for all in this land.

The no War, it can only be postponed to blown up. Women with baby on tried to reach the advantage of others." Machiavelli, The Prince

SONDAG, 10 SEPTEMBER 198

South African
Police
offering accomodation
to students since
1976
in
SOWETO

CELL
5

a. The grand "Bazar". Roasting of brochettes.

b. Casablanca Berber market

Note facial
tattoos;
I. forehead —
II. under chin.

21
LA MANO

41
LA ROSA

I. amber beads above.

II. Berber Woman    Vendor of spices

III. Detail of facial tattoos

POTIONS OF LUST

40
EL ALACRAN

PERVERSION

D'UN

EL BORRACHO

EL SOLDADO

Stark, Raving Mad and armed to the teeth

LA MUERTE

كوكا كولا

*Coca-Cola*

ماركات مسجلة

صودا / خلاصتها عصير نباتي

four hours and twelve positions in the...

"Hôtel Amour" an unmiraculate conception and...

The now famous... Perversion Sexuelle d'une adolescente.

This is not a preposition. Just put your feet-up, kick back and watch the sweaty bun away.

Long Live the ideals of Liberté Egalité and Safari

Hôtel

Amour

yes, we have wings... but some don't know why...

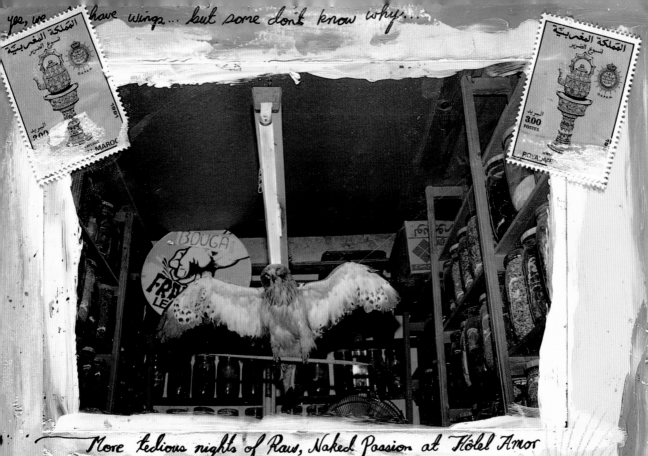

More tedious nights of Raw, Naked Passion at Hôtel Amor

She was a hunter-gatherer and a victim and carrier.
The Sex Killer of Room 416

Hôtel Amor

Devant la plus belle Plage

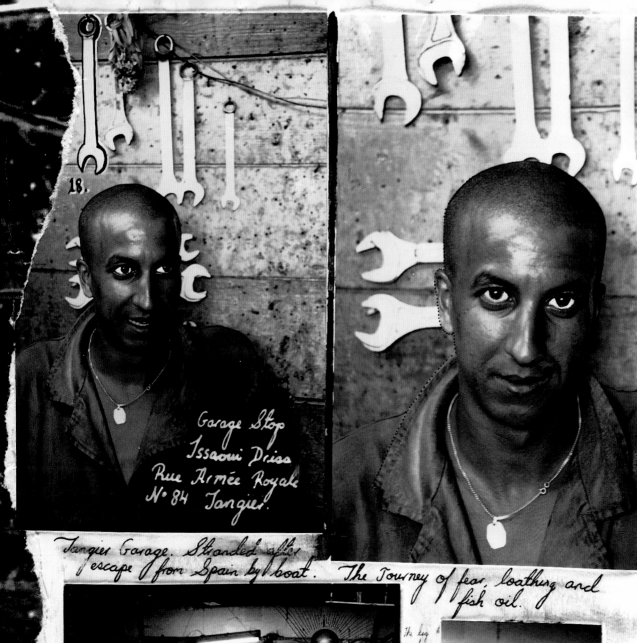

18.

Garage Stop
Issaoui Driss
Rue Armée Royale
Nº 84 Tangier.

Tangier Garage. Stranded after escape from Spain by boat.

The Journey of fear, loathing and fish oil.

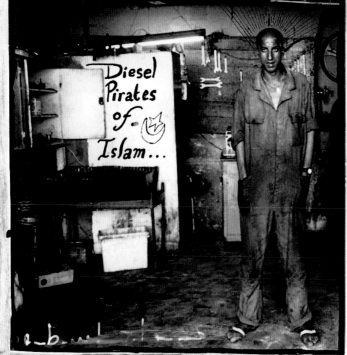

Diesel
Pirates
of. ☪
Islam...

The Northern gate of Africa.
Tangier 1991

زنقة 25

ZANQAT 25

البريد

POSTE

*Fathers of black magic #1*

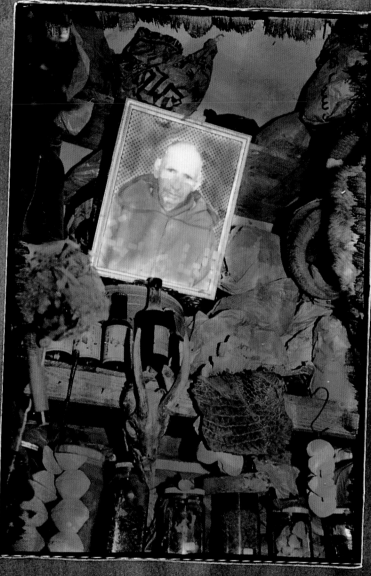

*Fathers of black magic #2*

Liberté, Egalité, Safari

"Wish You Were Here! Greetings from Southern Spain"

"The Big Blue" in southern Spain.

Dan Eldon "The Great Desert" North Africa

July 1991

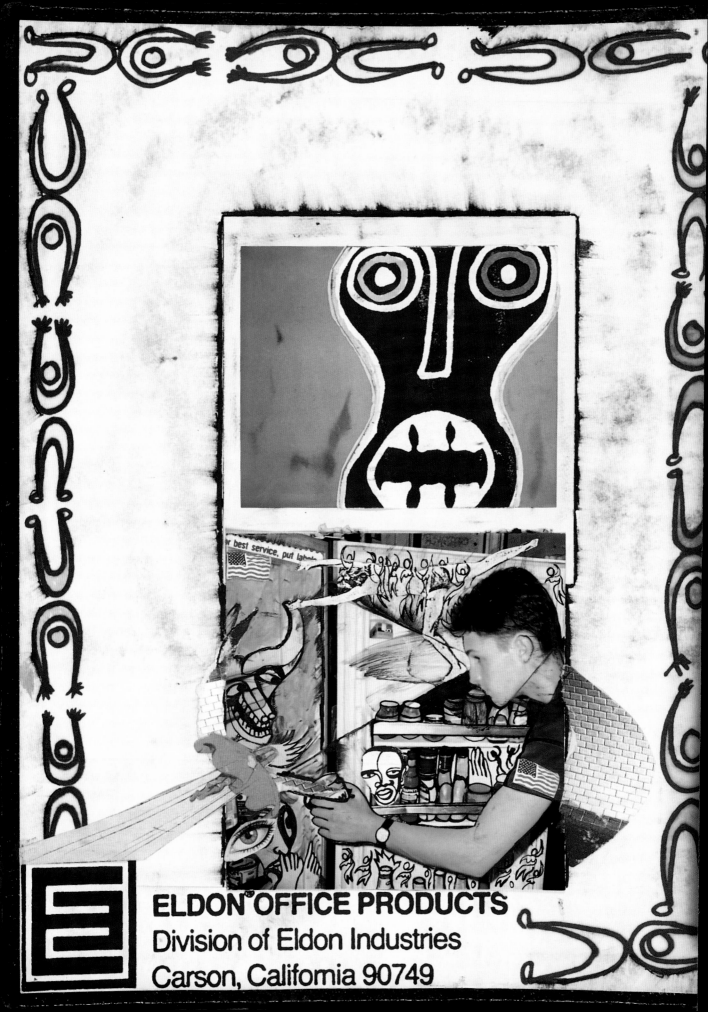

ELDON® OFFICE PRODUCTS
Division of Eldon Industries
Carson, California 90749

# NEW YORK

NEW YORK ON 50 BRAIN CELLS A DAY

NEW YORK ON 50

SEPTEMBER EIGHTEENTH 1988

sky

SKY.

NEW YORK

ON 50 BRAIN CELLS A DAY.

NEW YORK ON 50 BRAIN CELLS A DAY - NEW YORK ON 50 BRAIN CELLS
A DAY - NEW YORK ON 50 BRAIN CELLS A DAY - NEW YORK ON 50 BRAIN CELLS A

I have 3 things
here —
① My house,
(400$ per month)
② My book
(100 pages)
③ My Head.
(2 eyes)

I share my
house with a
room
I'll
my b_____th
o_____
my head is

MY OWN

New York on
50
Brain cells a
DAY.

a guide book.

# New York on 50 Brain Cells a Day...

## A Guidebook.

# BLOW YOURSELF UP

Great gift idea!

BLOW YOURSELF UP

# BLOW YOURSELF UP

WHITE BLOWUPS TOO!!

THOU SHALT
NOT CHUCK
STUFF OUT
THE WINDOW

blown up

BLOW YOURSELF UP

02484

0 77884

# KIZUNGU - ZUNGU

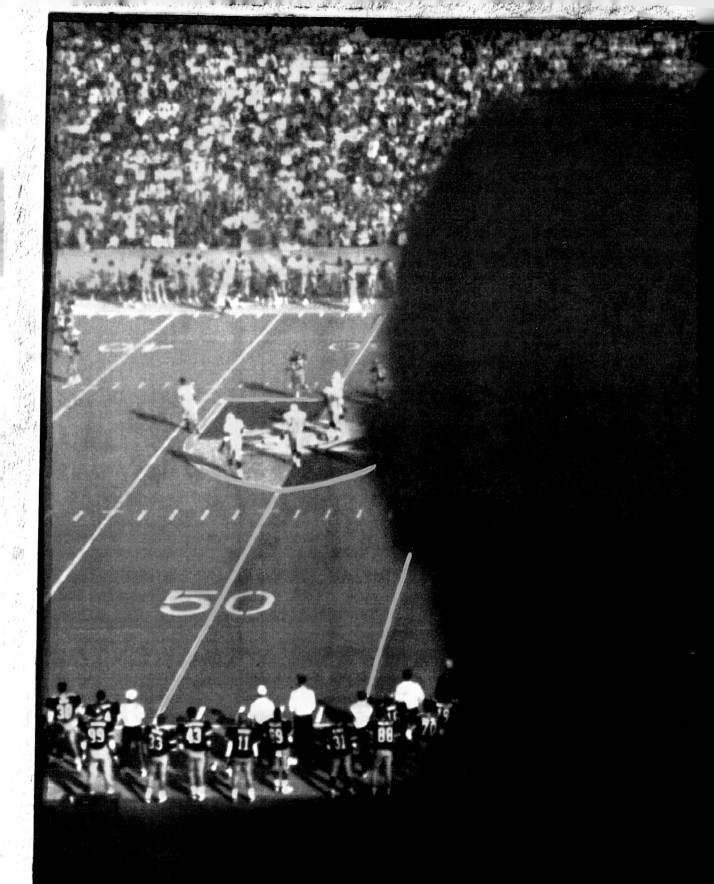

West Point. Army cadet football

game - V.I.P. stand. Officer's Head.

# DEZIREE SAFARIS

TEAM "Deziree" free at last "Voyages - the Search for clean water in a swamp

"Energy, sincerity, clarity of vision, creativity"

Mission Statement for... Safari as a Way of Life.

"To explore the unknown and the familiar, distant and near,
~ look for solutions - not problems ~
and to record in detail with the eyes of a child, any beauty, (of the flesh or otherwise) horror, irony, traces of utopia or Hell. Select your team with care, but when in doubt, take on new crew and give them a chance. But avoid at all costs fluctuations of sincerity with your best people."

It is therapeutic to apply a well toned beautiful naked body onto ones own flesh at least twice a day in tropical or non tropical climes.

NOTE: There is little difference between being lost and exploring.

create. Avoid eating nasty food when the taste can easily be improved by sauces. It is foolish and hazardous not to dance in Africa. some Sauces and clean water.

The most important part of vehicle maintenance is clean windows so if you are broken down, you will enjoy the beauty of the view. Also, ensure that electronic devices to play music are properly serviced. The more music you like the happier you will be.

New York London Nairobi Rome Yokohama Paris

The fleet USS Arabella and the HMS Deziree sets sail from Selmia Harbour.

# DEZIREE SEX SAFARIS

LA SANDIA

LA CALAVERA

EL ALACRAN

"find Clarity of Vision"

what is the difference between exploring and being

**Hosea**

**Joel**

Your old men shall
dream dreams, your
young men shall see
visions. *Joel 2: 28.*

**Amos**

Seek good, and not
evil, that ye may live.
*Amos 5: 14.*

29

# DEZIREE SAFARIS

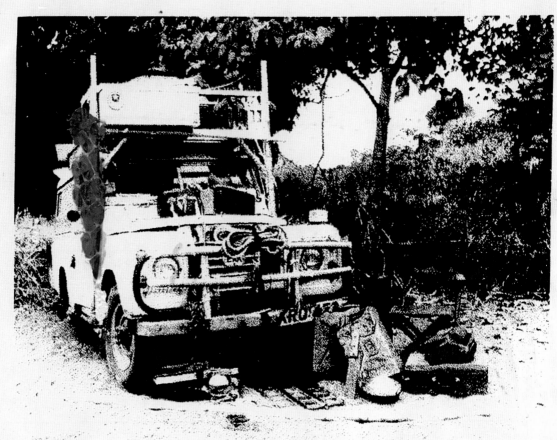

*what is the difference between exploring and being lost?*
*"The Journey is the Destination..."*

*"free at last" Safari Company...*

TEAM DEZIREE
★ BOX 53441 ★
NAIROBI, KENYA.

New York  London  Nairobi  Rome  Yokohama  Paris

The very
sea did
rot - o christ
we stuck
nor breath
nor motion
as idle
as a
painted
ship
upon a
painted
ocean.

The very
deep did rot o christ
That ever this
should be.
Yea, slimy things
did crawl with
legs, upon the slimy sea.

water, water everywhere,
and all
the board
did shrink

Water, water
everywhere
nor any
drop to
drink -

Samuel
Taylor
Cookridge

76 CASABLANCA - S/S Djenné de la Compagnie Paquet

DEZIRE SAFARI

.37 CASABLANCA                    Parc Lyautey

The Wines and Messing Committee wish to remind members that there is a book.
in the diningroom for members' comments - good or bad: preferably the former.
It is almost unbelievable, but it is true that there have been instances of
childish vandalism in the book also an obscenity: the Committee are appalled
and trusts that this will never happen again.

FUCK off -

*Livingstonia Beach*

The lost swimming crew of the Safari; the unlucky ones

*Malawi*

*Zambia Ballet Picnic*

G. Bown

"¡NO PASSARAN!"

preservation. The fact is that a man who wants to act virtuously in every way necessarily comes to grief among so many who are not virtuous. Therefore if a prince wants to maintain his rule he must learn how not to be virtuous, and to make ~~~~~~~~~~~~ not according to

THE BLUE DWARF

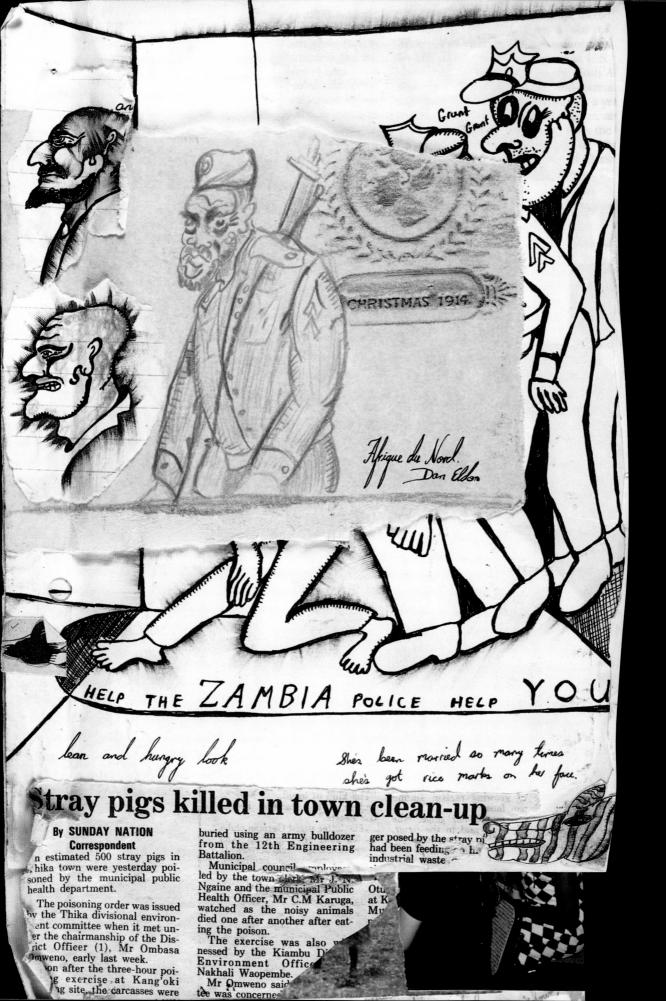

CHRISTMAS 1914

Afrique du Nord.
Dan Eldon

Grunt
Grunt

HELP THE ZAMBIA POLICE HELP YOU

lean and hungry look

She's been married so many times
she's got rice marks on her face.

# Stray pigs killed in town clean-up

**By SUNDAY NATION**
**Correspondent**

n estimated 500 stray pigs in
hika town were yesterday poi-
soned by the municipal public
health department.

The poisoning order was issued
by the Thika divisional environ-
ent committee when it met un-
er the chairmanship of the Dis-
rict Officer (1), Mr Ombasa
mweno, early last week.

on after the three-hour poi-
g exercise at Kang'oki
g site, the carcasses were

buried using an army bulldozer
from the 12th Engineering
Battalion.

Municipal council employes
led by the town clerk, Mr J. N.
Ngaine and the municipal Public
Health Officer, Mr C.M Karuga,
watched as the noisy animals
died one after another after eating the poison.

The exercise was also w
nessed by the Kiambu D
Environment Office
Nakhali Waopembe.

Mr Omweno said
tee was concerned

ger posed by the stray p
had been feeding h
industrial waste

Otu
at K
M

"There was not one single thing that he found undeserving of contempt."

a.

b.

Plate XVI. Dan Eldon. 1991.

# Jurkish Brothel

Three second fuse of desire

a nervous twist of lust invisible

SHE LAUGHED LIKE A GIANT HAND

TICKLED HER

Voluptious spasm.

must be rationed. — Lenin

ONE HUNDRED MILLION

over the past one hundred years, one hundred million people died from war.

By Dan Eldon, Reuters

Origin of Inequality among Men.

"only the dead have
seen the end
of War."

Plato

The Night of a Thousand
Eyes

REMEDY

# THE DEAD BOY

**Team Deziree**

We arrived late but it did not matter, we were two hours early. We queued up in the popular Malawi style whereby you get inside. The person infront of you gets even closer to the table. Really ......... their way ........... saying that ......... sacred a New York right due ......... no, they were forced to pay ......... the Kwacha entrance fee.

Our first impression was, wow, what a lot of Drunk ......... but we soon realized that ......... were twice as many as we first thought. The most notable of the drunkards was a man called Skull, a Zambian national, a country not altogether unfamous for their drinking habits.

Amy found a young ruffian who had tried to jump a barbed wire fence, but his crotch was caught and shreded on the sharp barbs. He lay on the ground, writing chipuku, the beer of good cheer, as blood clotted around his mid-section.

Amy is a sympathetic person, (some perhaps would say too sympathetic) and she decided that the fellow needed medical attention, and not the attention that the leering passers-by were giving generously. She teacher ......... than a police officer who was ......... it less than interested ......... far less than no ......... Amy battled with ......... boy of the Kamuzu ......... administrat. She demmanded an ......... Stadium and a doctor for the boy. She voulenteered Dezire to ......... as an ......... to transport the body to hospital. In the end, some of his friends ......... him and drenched him in water.

7

enjoy!

"enjoy the
dead
boy."

dead boy

"we should tell his
mother."

8

# DEZIREE SEX SAFARIS

New York London Nairobi Rome Yokohama Paris

Here is the scene Burke comes to Kenya to see Dan and Akiko ends up with his best friend Lengai. Akiko also come out to see Dan but then ends up

VINOS

The first meeting of the MALAWI MAFIA FAMILY, the Kamuzinis

AMY "the Razor Eldon"

NOW THATS A FINE LOOKING CHICK

at Mama Pirinis delfin Pasta place in Blantyre

I love you like a sister but I would stamp you out like an ant if you betray me

Aieee I'm Shot!

BOOM!

you eat my brains.

"Strangelove"

feeling good was good enough for me ...

Tanzania,
Mikumi
Nat. Park.

The illegal campsite in Mikumi National Park. The next morning, we bus out through a newly made road. Made in fact by Dr. Croze and I.

Dedicated to all those who lost their lives during the drama

Campsik with some members of Team Dezilee.

Escape from Mikumi Nat. Park.

ME GOT THE AGONY
SHE GOT THE REMEDY

HISTORY OF MY FACE
1981 — 1991

EL CAMAR

ILFORD XP2 400 DX 135 36

FILM FOR COLOR SLIDES
Kodak
Kodachrome
200
L 135-36
36 EXP
DX 35 mm
FOR COLOR PRINTS
5-24
4 EXP 100

Gold
FILM FOR COLOR PRINTS
135-24
4 EXP 100

Kodak
Gold
FILM FOR COLOR PRINT
GA 135-36
36 EXP

Kodak
EKTAR
1000
24 EXP
CJ 135-24
35mm
FILM FOR COLOUR PRINTS
L POUR COULEUR

135-36
NEOPAN
1600
Professional
FILM FOR BLACK & WHITE PRINTS

Gold
FILM FOR COLOR PRINTS
GA 135-24
24 EXP 100

ILFORD
XP2
400
DX 135 36

Kodak
EKTAR
1000
24 EXP
CJ 135-24
35mm
FILM FUR FARBBILDER
PELLICOLA PER A COLORI

Kodak
Gold
FILM FOR COLOR PRINT

ILFORD
XP
400
DX 135

XP2
400
DX 135 36

23

ROTTING

**BODIES**

Scenic View, Arizona.

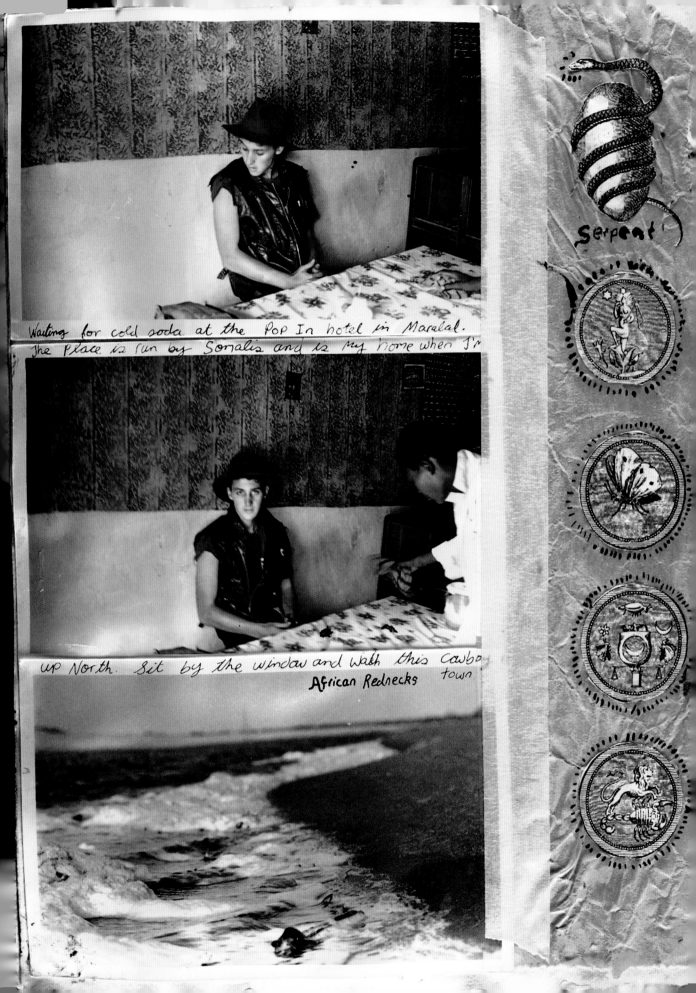

Waiting for cold soda at the Pop In hotel in Maralal.
The place is run by Somalis and is my home when I'm

Up North. Sit by the window and watch this Cowboy
**African Rednecks** town.

Serpent

ドクターハンス

THE PRO-
TRUD-
ING

NAIL WILL BE

HAMMERED INTO

 PLACE.

① ② ③

Nelson turns
blind eye to
telescope.

} we exist somewhere

fig I Planes of

November 2nd
1991
Los Angeles.

Interesting facts
of the day: "Your mother is
so ugly tha[t] ... the tide
won't lake ...

Late Oct. 1991. Desert

Photos right: from the ill-
fated expedition to view the
thousands of yellow umbrellas
planted in the desert north of
Los Angeles. We arrived in the
middle of the worst storm in
recent history. The night that
we went ... one m...
umbrella...
as up...
wind
us...

yellow umbrellas.

"Neema"
"Kadogo" "Sweetie,"
"Sugar,"
"Shifta"
"Giza,"
"Makaa"
"Somali,"
"Toto"

Neema
Ali,"

Amy applies mud to
Samburu mom

Neema, the Somali village girl in Shaka

Sudan, the lion from L. A. in Amboseli.

28 MAY 1992

TWO SCISSORS

TRADE MARK
GEISH
BRAND

NET WEIGHT
125 GRAMS
PRODUCTION: AUGUST 1991
EXPIRY    AUGUST 1993
تاريخ الانتاج اغسطس ١٩٩١
تاريخ الانتهاء اغسطس ١٩٩٣

SARDINES
IN VEGETABLE OIL SALT ADDED
PACKED FOR
NOZAKI & CO., LTD.
TOKYO, JAPAN    PRODUCT OF THAILAND

LANGA
GROC
55

11:41:16

# CARNIVAL

SALSA

LA ARAÑA

EL SOLDADO

LA ESTRE

LA CALAVERA

LA CAMPANA

EL CANTA

LA PALMA

LA MACETA

EL AR

EL GORRITO

LA BOTA

EL DIABLITO

LA DAMA

LA SANDIA

EL VALIE

# PARA LA MUSICA LATINA!

# FESTIVAL!

EL CAZO

46 EL SOL

47

48

49

50 EL PESCADO

EL VENADO

51 LA PALMA

GALLO
Don Clemente

LA RANA

32 EL MUSICO

S A M B A !

EL PAJARO

LA ROSA

38 EL APACHE

EL MELON

# MARILYN Y NEEMA!!

above:
Riding in
Dewree in
Nairobi with
Khadogo
July.

Left: Coast
Trip, Diani

Bottom: Matatu
ride with
our friends
Below: Kikuku
shots
G Bam

Left: Neema
fresh and
clean from the
shower in
Eva's house
July '92

UBLE HAPPINESS

達

火柴

AFETY MATCHES

中國製造 MADE IN CHINA

*Below, Roberta's ranch, Northern Kenya*

Stockholm, Sweden ~ in "our boat"

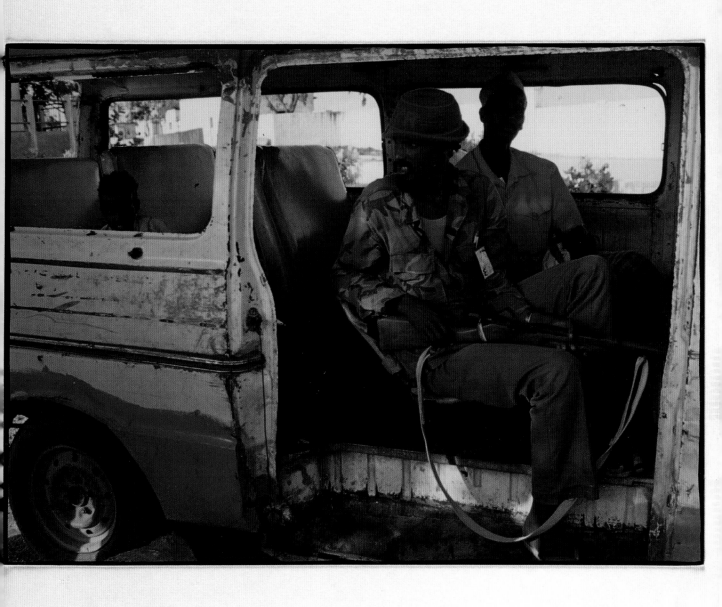

In thanking all the people who helped shape Dan's perspective on the world, I have tried to imagine who he would have pointed out as being the most significant. I know his thanks would have gone first to his father, Mike, who worked patiently with Dan, aged six, to create magical stamp albums. That year, he also taught him how to use his first camera, instilling in him a lifetime habit of picture taking. The two shared an outrageous sense of humor, the ability to make puns in a variety of languages, and a strange inability to carry a tune.

Artists and photographers were frequent visitors to our Nairobi home: the famous duo Angela Fisher and Carol Beckwith were our most popular, lending not only tips on shutter speeds, but more importantly, teaching Dan how to simultaneously befriend and photograph people of diverse cultures. Photographer David Coulson and intrepid explorer Wilfred Thessiger were other early influences, along with Liza MacKay, who, together with Doria Block, were the first people to take Dan's art seriously.

Dan loved Kati Korppijaakko, then Art Director of *Mademoiselle* magazine, who bravely hired Dan, aged only seventeen, to work in her office. It was Kati and her lively young staff who gave Dan free use of the photocopier and encouraged him to believe in his talent. When Dan decided to found

# ACKNOWLEDGMENTS

Student Transport Aid, he was assisted by friends around the world, including Adrian House, who encouraged Dan to go on a great safari across Africa. It was an adventure that was to affect the lives of fourteen young people, who became some of Dan's closest friends and most patient subjects. He shared a special bond with each one of the multinational members of Team Deziree: Eiji Shumizu, Akiko Tomioka, Chaka Chaka, Roko Belic, Marte Rambourg, Jeff Worden, Chris Nolan, Lengai Croze, Ryan Bixby, Hayden Bixby, Robert Gobright, Jeff Gettleman, Eli Tatum (chief crepe-cook), and his fifteen-year-old sister, Amy.

Dan treasured his childhood friends, most of whom are featured in his journal pages. They include Marilyn Kelly, who appears frequently, first as a child of twelve, last as a gorgeous young woman of eighteen; Soya Gecaga, Robi Ancilotti, Phoebe Vreeland, Saskia Geissler, Anselm and Katrinika Croze, Laure Diaz, the Weisel brothers, Mikey G, Claire Johnson, Daire O'Reilly, Jean Marc Andre, Pierre Burton, Jonathan Seale, Annathea Henton, Carolyn Roumeguere, Carla Benson, Patrick Falconer, Amy Branch, Mike White, Long Westerlund, Jeff Wordon, Dawn and Darla Granger, Lara Leakey, Petra and Tara Fitzgerald, Andrea Lukasavitch, Guillaume Bonn, Neema Ali, and Dan's adopted Masai brother, Peter Lekarian.

Throughout Dan's brief career, journalist Maryanne Fitzgerald acted as a mentor and special friend to a young man she knew shared her humanitarian objectives. Dan's "photographer's eye" was first spotted by Sam Ouma, a brilliant photojournalist with the *Nation* newspaper in Kenya. Executive director Geoffrey Dudman encouraged Dan to aspire to be "another Fellini." As a young photographer in Somalia, Dan attached himself to talented veteran journalists and photojournalists, trailing after Corinne Dufka, Aiden Hartley, Andy Hill, and many others who generously shared tips with a rookie. The Nairobi Reuters Bureau Chief Jonathan Clayton took a chance on Dan by giving him a job as a proper stringer, and Reuters London staffers Pat Benic and Greg Bros patiently talked him through many difficult assignments. Dan was first inspired by one of Africa's legendary cameramen, Mohamed Amin, and later learned persistence and determination from another, Mohammed Shaffi, the only survivor of the tragic incident on July 12. Dan shared many challenges of life in Somalia— and the final moments before his death—with his friends and colleagues, Anthony Macharia and Hos Maina of Reuters, and Hansi Krauss of the Associated Press.

I know Dan would want a special mention of his oldest friend, Lengai Croze, who, as a tow-headed seven-year-old, protected Dan from class bullies, and, as a dashing young man, accompanied him on many safaris across Africa, coaxing Deziree to take on "just one more hill."

After Dan's death on July 12, 1993, I have to take over the thanks, first acknowledging the kind support of Maia Gregory, who was the first to help me organize the material necessary for a book based on Dan's journal pages. I am grateful to the memory of Anita Diamant, who believed so passionately in this project; to Kati Korppijaakko, now art director for *Glamour* magazine, who photocopied scores of journal pages as I wept beside her; and to Maryesta Carr, who nurtured my body and spirit. My love and thanks go to Mike Eldon, who told me never to give up; to Gaby, Ruth, and the memory of Bruno Eldon for their continuous encouragement; and to my inspirational parents, Russell and Louise Knapp, who made it possible for me to continue when I thought I couldn't go on.

I treasure the memory of Ruth Schaffner, the courageous director of the Watatu Gallery in Nairobi, who produced "The Show Goes On," the first retrospective of Dan's art, photography, and journal pages, together with her assistant, Rob Burnett. Leslie Wright of the Cedar Rapids Museum of Art organized the first American exhibit of Dan's work at her museum, which is now the permanent home for Dan's archives. I am deeply grateful to Dr. and Mrs. Semans, who funded the first American exhibition of journal pages at Duke University. It was there that Alex Harris asked permission to publish a selection of pages in his stunning magazine, *Doubletake*.

The article was seen by a young Saatchi & Saatchi advertising executive, Marcel Cairo, who courageously took a year off to research Dan's life for a feature film. Craig Walker saw the piece and contributed dozens of art and photographic books to help me understand Dan's work. Lisa Henson, then president of Columbia Pictures, read the *Doubletake* piece and decided Dan's story had to be told. My thanks to Naomi Despres and producer Janet Yang for joining forces with Lisa Henson and me to make a feature film inspired by the journals; and to Michael Costigan for his energy, creativity and enthusiasm in realizing that dream. To Bruce Smith, Russel Fischer, Marcel Cairo, and Jan Sardi, I offer my heartfelt gratitude for their determined exploration of thousands of journal pages as they struggled to unravel the mysteries hidden within. I have been fortunate to have friends like Chris Conrad, Rebecca and David Flaeter, Martin Jarvis, and Ros Ayres, who befriended me on my arrival in Los Angeles, and who encouraged me to continue, no matter what.

Shortly after Dan's death, Debbie Gaiger created the book and exhibition, *Images of Conflict,* based on photographs by the three photographers who died together in Somalia. The exhibition, supported by Reuters Managing Editor Mark Wood and Associated Press Chiefs Lou Boccardi and Myron Belkind, has traveled to eight countries. Scores of people have been vital to the success of the events, including Professor Maristella Lorch of the Italian Institute, broadcasters Tom Brokaw and Dan Rather, Michael Buerk, Sir Brian Urquhart, and the presidents of Kenya, Cyprus, and Ireland. Canon John Oates of St. Brides Church, the famous journalists' church on London's Fleet Street, has been a continuing source of inspiration for our entire family. It was Canon Oates who offered to dedicate a young tree in the courtyard of his church in Dan's name, which also commemorates the "tortured people of Somalia." Veteran photographer Eddie Adams, one of Dan's heroes, has been unfailingly supportive of our attempts to inspire and encourage young photographers to pursue their highest objectives. Young photographer Patrick Whalen has been resourceful in helping me digitize Dan's collection of journal pages.

The book would not have been possible without the dedicated efforts of my hardworking agent, Jane Dystel; Steve Oliver, who painstakingly photographed the pages represented in this book; the staff of Chronicle Books, especially Karen Silver, who patiently guided me throughout the publishing process, and Laura Lovett, for designing a book that would make Dan proud.

There are countless other people around the world to whom Dan and I owe our appreciation. Forgive us for not including your name. You know who you are.

My greatest thanks are reserved for Annie Barrows, who recognized that Dan had an important message for people around the world. Annie is the true editor of Dan's journals; a feisty, funny, creative, and persistent individual, whose enlightened spirit mirrors Dan's and utterly pervades this book.

My final words are for my inspiration, Amy Louise Eldon, Dan's little sister, his favorite model, cherished confidante, and dearest friend. It is to Amy that this book is lovingly dedicated.

# DEZIREE SEX SAFARIS

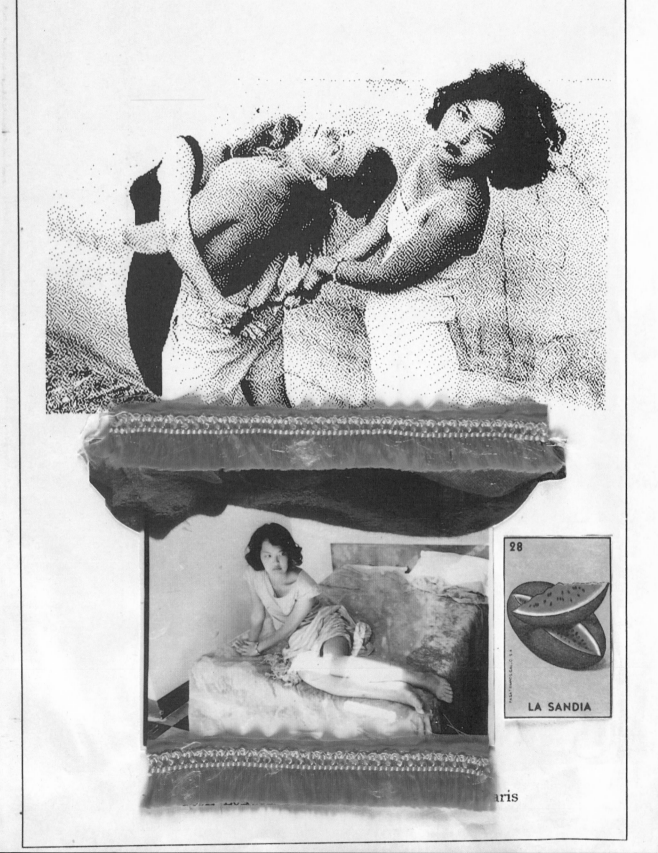

28

LA SANDIA